My Money Book & Journal

Managing Money & Credit

My Money Book & Journal

Managing Money & Credit

J. McCrary

Community Services Press

Mechanicsburg, Pennsylvania

COMMUNITY SERVICES PRESS

Community Services Press
5133 Kylock Road
Mechanicsburg, PA 17055

www.communityservicespress.com

Printed in the United States of America
18 17 16 15 14   1 2 3 4 5

ISBN 13: 978-1-938620-05-8

Acknowledgments and thanks

Money for education (pp. 18-20) was reviewed and improved by Frank E. Basehoar, college planning consultant of Mechanicsburg, PA.

Money Math (pp. 37-40) and mathematics throughout the book were reviewed and lesson plans created by Kathleen Barber, M.Ed.

The Pennsylvania Banker Association's Retired Bankers Committee members reviewed the book and offered valuable input.

Jocelyn Rivera of Mid Penn Bank in Camp Hill, PA, reviewed and improved *Banks & My Money* (pp. 23-30)

My Money Book & Journal was written by J. McCrary
Editing by Melanie Mallon, Mallon Editorial Services
Illustrations by Bonnie Bright, Bright Illustration
Cover design by Gary Smith, Performance Design
Interior layout by Michael Vezo, Westcom Associates

Contents

Benjamin Franklin (1706-1790), one the most famous and beloved founders of the United States, was an author, inventor, scientist and diplomat. Though he helped write both the Declaration of Independence and the American Constitution, Franklin is best known for his wise sayings, which are as valuable now as they were 250 years ago. Franklin's quotes about money are sprinkled throughout *My Money Book & Journal.*

Money Basics

You have been given *My Money Book & Journal* by your bank or by someone who cares about your financial future. The information on the next 57 pages will help you manage your money and build and protect your credit.

My Money Book & Journal asks you to become involved personally in your journey to financial literacy. As you give honest answers to questions about your money habits, you will get a handle on your money-spending triggers. By setting savings goals and figuring out what you *really* earn and spend, you'll create a budget.

You will unravel the mystery of paycheck deductions and discover the advantages of ATMs, automatic deposits and deductions, and different types of bank accounts. As you learn about credit ratings and identity theft, you will also learn how to manage credit and debit cards safely.

The glossary on pages 62–63 is a quick reference to money terms that you'll need to remember. Math questions will help you keep tabs on your financial literacy level. The journal section will help you track your income, expenses, savings, and debts. As you fill out the money journal, you will continue to develop and strengthen your money- and credit-management skills, and you will be on the path to financial success.

Earning Money

Whether your money comes from odd jobs you do for family and friends, your allowance, gifts, or a wage-paying job, it's all called *income*.

When you officially join the ranks of tax-paying citizens, you may be shocked at the difference between your *gross income*, the amount you actually earn, and your *net income*, known as your take-home pay. The difference between the two is called *withholding*, or payroll deductions.

Some of your withholding is for federal, state, and local income taxes. As a taxpayer, you pay for schools, the armed services, and fire and police departments. Your money builds roads and bridges, fuels city buses, runs the court system and prisons, and sends astronauts into space.

When you are first hired, you are given a worksheet called a *W4 Form* to fill out. Federal and state income tax deductions will be calculated from the information on this form. You want the right amount of taxes to be deducted from your paycheck throughout the year so that you won't have too much withheld or owe taxes and penalties on April 15, tax day.

Don't panic! Federal and state income taxes are quite small amounts when your earnings are low. As you earn more, your tax *bracket*, or the percentage of your income that you pay in taxes, increases.

The hardest thing in the world to understand is income tax.
—Albert Einstein

Depending on where you live, local income taxes and unemployment taxes may also be deducted. These taxes are usually very small percentages of your income.

Don't forget to file your taxes each year. Most people get money back from the government.

Money is also deducted from your paycheck for Social Security and Medicare. These deductions may be listed separately on your paycheck stub or be jointly identified as *FICA* (Federal Insurance Contributions Act).

Social Security is best known as retirement income, but it is also your insurance policy while you're not old enough to qualify for retirement. If you become sick or injured and aren't able to work, you may qualify for Social Security disability. If you do qualify, you will receive monthly payments based on a percentage of your earnings. Social Security survivors' benefits help support your children and other dependents if you die.

Medicare is basic health insurance for most people who receive Social Security.

Almost everybody in the workforce pays for Social

> Taxes are dues that we pay for the privilege of membership in an organized society.
> —President Franklin Delano Roosevelt

Security programs. In 2014, Social Security tax is 12.4% of your salary, and Medicare tax is an additional 2.9%. You and your employer each pay one-half of the total FICA tax owed on your income. If you work for yourself or are an independent contractor, you pay the entire FICA tax yourself.

Let's review employee benefits. When your employer offers insurance coverage as a benefit to employees (such as health, life, vision, dental, and disability insurance), you usually pay part of the cost if you choose to enroll in the program. Your employer will contribute a portion of the *premium*, or cost, and you will pay the rest.

Your employer may also offer you optional benefits and payroll deductions. One desirable option is a 401(k) program, a savings plan for your retirement. Not all employers offer these programs, and usually you must work at your job for several months or a year before you're allowed to participate.

There are three major benefits in joining 401(k) programs:

- Your taxable income is reduced by the amount of your contribution, which means your taxes are reduced (with limits).
- Your money automatically goes into savings before you can be tempted to spend it.
- Your employer may match a percentage of your savings and deposit it into your account. That's **free** money!

A 401(k) program is designed for your retirement, and you should consider the money to be *very* long-term savings. The money belongs to you, and some programs allow you to borrow against your 401(k) savings and pay yourself back over several years. You can also withdraw money if you are willing to pay penalties or if you are in certain qualifying circumstances such as buying your first house. Borrowing or withdrawing 401(k) money is not something to undertake lightly. The government and nonprofit organizations have other retirement programs that are similar in some ways.

The government knows that wait staff, musicians, hair

Sample Paycheck Stub

Employee: Abby Dinero **SSN:** 123-45-8690

Pay Period 5/2/2010–5/8/2010

Earnings and Hours

Number of Hours	Hourly Rate	Current Earnings	Year To Date Earnings
21:25	$7.50	$159.38	$1,042.53

Taxes

	Current	Year To Date
City Withholding	- $2.55	-$16.68
Federal Withholding	-$15.99	-$104.25
Social Security Employee	- $9.88	-$64.64
Medicare Employee	- $2.31	-$15.31
State Withholding	- $4.89	-$32.04
State Unemployment Withholding	- $0.10	-$0.63
Total Withholding	-$35.72	-$233.55
Net Pay	$123.66	$ 808.98

stylists, and many others earn a big portion of their income through tips. The IRS (Internal Revenue Service), the money-collecting arm of the federal government, *audits*, or checks, tip records at restaurants if they believe tips are not being reported. The IRS may also ask to see your tip records as well.

TIP is an acronym for To Insure Promptness

The National Restaurant Association posts these guidelines for anyone earning tips:

- All tips are taxable. Report 100% of your tips!
- You must record your tips daily. You may be audited.
- You must report cash tips as well as credit card tips to your employer each month.
- Not reporting your tips *is* a big deal.

If you receive shared or pooled tips from co-workers, you are still expected to abide by these rules.

Spending Money

Don't we all know how to spend money? Isn't that just natural? Not at all! Spending money *well* is an acquired skill.

Some of us are natural hoarders, and we become anxious when we have to make spending decisions.

Others are spendthrifts, and we blow through all the money that comes our way. We don't have a clue where it went, but we hope we had fun while it lasted. Unfortunately, we're often just broke!

A lucky few of us spend wisely. Some were taught by example—perhaps our parents gave us an allowance and spending responsibilities and helped us make good spending decisions. Unfortunately, most of us learn to be good spenders the hard way, by making expensive mistakes. At some point, we learn to tell the difference between what we need and what we want.

> Beware of little expenses;
> a small leak will sink a great ship.
> —**Benjamin Franklin**

There are some basic guidelines to spending well.

Look closely at your small but routine expenses. Benjamin Franklin's "small leaks" quote is as valid today as it was over 250 years ago.

What does it cost to buy a bagel and a small coffee every day on the way to work or school (not counting the calories, of course)? No, it's not $4.00. This little breakfast snack habit can cost you $1,000 each and every year. If you had $1,000 in your hands now, how would you like to spend it? Perhaps on new clothes, travel, or your education? Or would you rather let the money leak out of your pocket $4.00 at a time?

Consider how long it takes you to earn the money. A way to put your spending in perspective is to know how long you worked to earn the money you're about to spend. If you earn $8.00 per hour take-home pay, do you want to work thirty minutes just for your coffee and bagel? Maybe you could spend three minutes preparing 20 cents' worth of toast and coffee at home instead.

Imagine you want to buy a jacket on sale; it's a bargain, only $120 ($128 with tax), down from the full retail price of $240. Half price! Is it really a bargain, though, if you have to work sixteen hours or spend two months' allowance to buy it?

When we look at a big expense, the hours we work to pay for it can add up to days, weeks, months, or even years of our labor. Do you really want to work a whole year to pay for your car? You may be surprised how many people do just that, though they may never think of it that way. Instead they just think about the monthly payments.

Know how much discretionary income you have. *Discretionary income* is money left over when all your fixed expenses paid; you make choices about spending the leftover money. Fixed expenses are regular payments such as car loans and insurance, or perhaps your cell phone. As you gain responsibilities, you will owe rent, utilities, perhaps even student loan and other debt payments. These financial commitments get paid first, and the money you have left over is discretionary.

Since we hardly ever have all the discretionary income we would like, we learn to make choices. You decide whether you spend your food money on bagels and coffee on the way to school or instead prepare breakfast at home and put the difference into the bank. Learning to manage your discretionary income well is one of the most important steps you make to ensure financial success.

Reader, I wish thee health, wealth, happiness.
—Benjamin Franklin

Saving Money

What makes most people feel comfortable financially? You'd think it would be how much they earn, right? Instead, for many, it's the amount of money they have in savings. You can earn a million dollars per year and still feel desperately broke if you don't have any money in savings.

Unfortunately, saving money is a habit that many people never bother to learn.

Learning to save is not hard. When you understand a few simple concepts and practice them regularly, you will develop the skills to become a good saver. Once you begin to save regularly, your savings habit will keep you on the path to financial success.

A penny saved is a penny earned.
—Benjamin Franklin

Pay yourself first. Whenever you have money in your pocket or in your bank account, stash some of it away in your savings first—before you spend. The money will continue to belong to *you*—it won't belong to a restaurant or store owner instead. If you wait to save whatever money you have left over after you finish spending, your money will almost certainly be long gone first.

Wait to buy until you can afford to pay for it without borrowing. This concept has become popular again after many decades of being widely ignored. When credit was easy, people thought, "Why wait? I'll buy it now and pay later."

Yes, you want it now. Yes, it will probably still be there when you have enough money saved so that you can pay cash.

But think of saving money in terms of becoming independent and being in control of your life. You will find saving much easier and more fun if you don't convince yourself that you're being deprived.

Set long-term and short-term savings goals. When you save for a few weeks or months for something you want to do or buy, you've set a short-term savings goal. When you're saving over a period of years for a car, a house, college, retirement, or something else expensive, you have made a long-term goal.

Let's compare the two goals. Imagine $15 is rattling around in your pocket, you earn $60 per week flipping hamburgers, and you are dying for a certain pair of shoes that costs $100. You can probably reach your short-term goal in two to six weeks, depending on how much discretionary income you have and how you spend it.

Now imagine you've just turned fourteen years old and you have already negotiated with your parents for a car on your sixteenth birthday. Your parents promise you $3,000 for a car, but the kind of car *you* want will cost $5,000. Your long-term savings goal will be $2,000 within two years, which means you need to save $84 per month, or $19.23 per week.

> **If you would be wealthy, think of saving more than getting.**
> **—Benjamin Franklin**

You can set short-term savings goals even before you find what you want to buy. If you save $15 per week for clothing, for instance, you will always have money set aside for buying just what you want when you want it. Having money already saved also lets you spontaneously "save" money by buying an item on sale.

We will do savings goal exercises in chapter 4, Money Math.

Earn free money! Though free money sounds too good to be true, guess what? It really *is* true! If you open a savings account or buy a savings bond, you will earn *interest*, a percentage of your *principal*, the original deposit or bond purchase amount. Interest rates are based on a wide variety of factors, and they can vary from day to day on certain types of accounts. No matter what the rate is, though, it's still free money.

Saving money in a bank can be done in many ways, which we'll explore later. Most bank accounts are insured by the federal government, and they are very safe; your money is protected even if the bank goes bankrupt. Though the interest you earn is a low rate, it will grow via the magic of *compound interest*, which is interest earned on the interest you've *already earned* on your principal.

Investing in *securities*—stocks, bonds, and mutual funds—as part of your long-term savings is much riskier than depositing your money in a savings account. Risk means you may earn larger sums than the interest a bank pays, but you can also lose some or all of your money if the value of the security goes down. No guarantees or insurance programs protect you when you invest your money in securities.

> I made my first investment at age 11. I was wasting my life until then.
> **—Warren Buffet, American billionaire**

Stocks are ownership shares of actual corporations, and their value can vary wildly as the company's value and the stock market go up and down. Stock owners usually have the right to attend annual company meetings and vote on directors.

Bonds are interest-paying IOUs that companies and governments give investors in return for loans. Your school was probably built with bond money. Bonds can be bought and sold, but their values don't usually fluctuate as much as stocks' values.

Mutual funds are sold by organizations that research then buy and sell the stocks and bonds of publicly traded companies. When you buy shares in a mutual fund you are bying a share of a *portfolio,* or group of stocks or bonds.

Most 401(k) savings programs and many independent investors invest in mutual funds. Mutual funds often require very little money to start investing, and their risk levels vary widely.

Money for Education

Most high-school graduates continue their education by attending a four-year college, community college, or a technical school, all of which can cost mind-boggling sums of money. To give you the most options when you graduate, you and your family will want to start saving years in advance.

> The only thing more expensive than education is ignorance.
> —Benjamin Franklin

In addition to the savings accounts and savings bonds we've already discussed, special college savings programs can build your school funds even faster.

Every state in the U.S. offers a *529 plan* for college savings. The plan gives tax breaks to your parents and other relatives and friends when they deposit money into your college fund. For a small management fee, your money is invested so that it can grow faster than it might in interest-earning savings accounts. A 529 plan is very similar to a 401(k) plan; your family can choose from several different investment programs, some riskier than others.

Some states and private colleges offer prepaid tuition plans that allow families to pay for tuition in advance. Pay a year's tuition now and you get a year of tuition in the future, without the inevitable tuition increases. Prepaid planss have some drawbacks, though; your college choices are limited, and there may be investment risks.

Don't assume that public schools cost less than private ones. Out-of-state public college tuition can be as expensive as private school fees, plus, many private schools have expanded financial aid packages. Look at the total out-of-pocket costs for true comparisons.

Your high school guidance counselor, college-planning professionals, and financial aid officers can help you through the maze of options and forms. Beware of financial agencies that charge fees but have only a post office box, or that have a bait-and-switch small fee that suddenly increases as soon as you want additional information.

Don't forget the very best type of college money: ***free* money.** Start looking at grants and scholarships when you're a sophomore or junior. Your parents need to fill out the Free Application for Federal Student Aid (FAFSA), which determines your eligibility for federal and state grants, federal student loans, and many scholarships. Make sure your parents fill it out *every* year, because their financial circumstances may change. If you have an older brother or sister in college, you are more likely to qualify for financial aid.

Grants can be thousands of dollars per year—and they don't need to be repaid! Even if your family makes more than $100,000 annually, you may qualify for a grant once factors such as the number of children in your family are considered. Fill out the FAFSA early because most colleges have a limited amount of scholarship money to give away, and it's usually awarded on a first-come, first-served basis. Private colleges often require additional detailed financial forms. *Always* ask what's needed and when the information is due.

"Budget" comes from an old French word for purse, "bougette"

Scholarships are also available from fraternal organizations such as Elks and Rotary clubs, churches, community and private foundations, trade unions, and thousands of groups you can research on the Internet. Some have no income restrictions, and some can be renewed each year while you're in school. You can combine many small scholarships into surprisingly large sums of money.

When you've applied for every last grant and scholarship that's available and you still need money for school, you can borrow. Federal and private student loans account for more financial aid than all grants and scholarships combined.

Loans are definitely not "free" money, though. Whether or not you graduate or have a job, you must start repaying the loans six months after you leave school.

Student debt can grow fast, and it's easy for students to lose track of what they owe. According to the Project on Student Debt, 70% of the students graduating from four-year colleges in 2012 had student loan debt, averaging $29,400 per person. One million students and former students owe at least $40,000.

Budgeting

Virtually every organization and company in the world has a *budget*, or financial plan. A budget is a roadmap for earning, spending, borrowing, and saving. Not all individuals and families have created personal budgets, unfortunately. Simple ignorance keeps them from using this valuable tool, because most people don't realize how much a budget could save them or how much they actually spend.

The first step in creating a budget is to calculate your income, whether it comes from work, an allowance, or gifts. Next, track every expense. If your outgo exceeds your income, you're running a *deficit*, which is also known as going "in the hole." You need to cut expenses—or increase your income.

> Our necessities never equal our wants.
> —**Benjamin Franklin**

The goal is to have a *balanced budget* which means your income equals your expenses. Savings, charitable donations, and discretionary income all have their place in a balanced budget.

Let's look at two simple budgets. Richie is a high school freshman, and he receives an allowance that's meant to cover his expenses. He doesn't work, although his parents will give him additional money if he does household chores. It's clear that if Richie wants $7 or more per week in spending money, he will have to do some chores pretty regularly and maybe expand his work options.

High school senior Abby Dinero works in a fast food restaurant two nights after school and on weekends.

Richie's Monthly Budget

$60.00	**Monthly income**–allowance, and chores
	Monthly expenses
$10.00	Church offering
$25.00	Savings
$25.00	Discretionary income
$60.00	**Total monthly expenses**

(we looked at her paycheck stub on page 11.) Abby is responsible for gas and insurance for her car, her own clothes, cell phone, spending money, and saving for college. If Abby cuts back on driving she will have more discretionary income for clothes and fun.

Is your budget balanced? Go to page 45 and fill out the budget worksheet.

Abby's Monthly Budget

$556.40	**Monthly income**–(21 hours/wk @ $7.50/hr minus withholding)
	Monthly expenses
$ 30.00	Cell-phone bill (Abby's share)
$124.00	Gasoline (average of 30 miles/day)
$ 72.40	Automobile insurance
$250.00	College savings
$ 80.00	Discretionary income
$556.40	**Total monthly expenses**

Banks & My Money

Banks have been around for over 5,000 years. For thousands of years before money was invented, early banks guarded grain, salt, and farm animals as well as precious metals and jewels.

Today's banks are friendly and accessible, even though you can't store cows or wheat in their vaults. Most banks give you access to your money 24/7 via ATMs and online banking. Branches are located in supermarkets and other convenient spots, and many are open evenings and weekends. Banks are active in the community.

Bank Accounts

Depending on your savings goals and how often you plan to deposit and withdraw your money, you may need more than one type of bank account.

Checking accounts are for your everyday spending and bill-paying money. You can write paper checks or use debit cards to make purchases and withdraw cash from your account. Some checking accounts are "free," or without fees, and some charge fees. Some have restrictions or require minimum balances, but often your savings account and checking account balances can be combined to qualify for free accounts. Your banker will help you choose the type of account that suits your needs.

Most checking accounts don't earn interest. Interest-bearing checking accounts usually require a relatively high minimum balance, often thousands of dollars.

It's important to keep track of the amount of money in your checking account. If you write an overdraft, which means you spent more money than you have available in the account, you'll be embarrassed and possibly even get into trouble. At the very least, your bank will charge you a hefty fee for "insufficient funds" and bounce the check, which means the check will be sent back to the business or person to whom you wrote it.

Bouncing a check can get you into deeper trouble than just fees and a damaged credit rating. In the worst-case scenario, you could be prosecuted. To help prevent insufficient fund complications, banks offer overdraft protection, which we'll discuss in My Credit, chapter 3.

Keep an accurate ledger of your account as you spend your money, and you'll stay out of trouble. You'll receive a check ledger when you open your checking account and receive a box of paper checks. The check ledger will help you keep track of the checks you write, the money and checks you deposit, and your account balance. You should also keep track of all your debit card transactions on the ledger (more on debit cards in Banking Tools, page 28).

Here's Abby's checking account ledger:

DC Debit Card · ATM Teller Withdrawal · AD Automatic Deposit · AP Automatic Payment · BP Online Bill Pay · T Online or Phone Transfer

NUMBER OR CODE	DATE	TRANSACTION DESCRIPTION	PAYMENT, FEE WITHDRAWAL (-)	✓	FEE	DEPOSIT, CREDIT (+)	$ 310.00
T	5/9	transfer to savings	$ 250 00	✓		$	60 00
DC	5/11	Shell-gas	22 00	✓			38 00
DC	5/12	Rite-Aid	9 00	✓			29 00
AD	5/12	paycheck (5/2 - 5/8				123 66	152 66
1027	5/13	Never-Wreck Auto Ins (May bill)	72 40				80 26
ATM	5/13	Cash	20 00				60 26

Let's start at the top, and go over each transaction. The balance she carries forward from the previous page is $310, enough to make Abby's monthly transfer to a college fund savings account. She has to be very frugal over the next few days until her paycheck is automatically deposited. Abby uses her debit card to buy just enough gas to get back and forth to work and a few items at the drug store.

Her paycheck brings her balance back up from $29.00 to $152.66. The next day Abby mails a check to pay for her car insurance and deducts it from her account. Even though the check won't be deposited for a few days, she has committed the money to Never-Wreck and it's no longer available for her to spend. She has $80.26 to carry her to her next paycheck on the 19th. As you saw on Abby's budget (page 22), she has only $2.66 in discretionary spending per day.

Abby goes to her bank's ATM and withdraws $20.00 for spending money for the next week.

Notice the column for checkmarks that follows the "payment, fee, withdrawal" column on the ledger. Abby verified the transfer of $250 from her checking to savings account and checked it off; because her balance was so low, she went online and checked each transaction until her paycheck was safely deposited.

On page 39 in Money Math, you will see how you balance your checkbook using a monthly bank statement.

Even if you plan to exclusively use online banking and ATMS, it's important to learn how to handle and write paper checks. If someone pays you with a paper check, you need to endorse (sign) the check before you can cash or deposit it. Sign the back of the check at the top above the line that says "Do not write below this line." You can add "deposit only" and your account number for some extra safety.

There are some special rules for writing a paper check

correctly. Here is a check that Abby wrote to her insurance company; let's follow step by step:

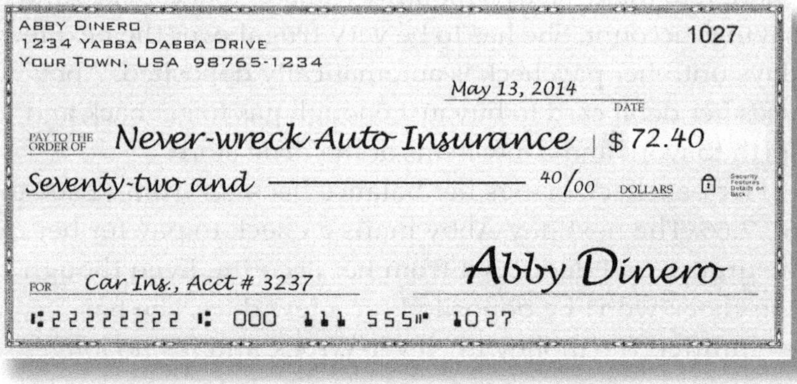

Fill out the date you are writing the check and the payee (the person or company you're paying). You write the amount twice. First, write the amount of the check numerically (Abby wrote $72.40). Write the amount on the next line in script, which prevents someone from easily increasing the amount (Seventy-two and------40/00 in this case). A long line from the dollar amount to the fractional cents at the end of the line also makes it harder for someone to change the amount.

Use the memo line to identify why you are writing the check, and if you're paying a bill, include the account number that appears on your bill. Make sure you sign the check.

It's important to understand the numbers at the bottom of the check. The number at the left between the ⑆ symbols is your bank's unique routing number. Your checking account number is next, in front of the ⑈ symbol. Your check number follows that symbol. You need to know the routing number and account number to receive direct deposits or make automatic payments.

In chapter 4, Money Math, you'll learn how to balance your checking account; that is, you'll see how to calculate the actual amount in your account.

Savings accounts are for money you plan to spend in the future. Banks pay you interest on the balance in your savings account, and in turn they charge interest to the people and businesses who borrow your money from the bank.

Before you open an account, ask about minimum deposit requirements and fees; sometimes these are waived for customers under the age of 18.

Money market accounts offer higher interest rates than checking accounts and sometime higher interest than you earn on your savings accounts. The bank invests your deposit in CDs, treasury bills or other loans, and high minimum balances are usually required. The bank often has a limit on the number of checks you can write or transfers you can make each month.

Certificates of Deposit, or CDs, are "time deposits" because you agree to leave your money in the bank for a specific period of time. The interest rate usually goes up as you increase the size and/or length of deposit. A $10,000 CD for a six-year period earns quite a bit more interest than a $500 CD for six months. You will be charged penalties if you cash in your CD before the *maturity date.*

Maximize the interest you earn by dividing your money among several types of accounts. You may want to keep a small amount of money in a non-interest-bearing checking account and use a savings account or money-market account for short-term savings and emergency funds, and when you have enough money saved, buy CDs for your long-term savings.

Your accounts are insured by the federal government for up to $250,000 per social security number or tax ID number per financial institution.

Banking Tools

ATMs, or automated teller machines, have revolutionized how people deal with money and banks within the last 25 years. You can make withdrawals, deposits, check your account balances, transfer funds between accounts, and buy U.S. Postal Service stamps 24 hours a day—the ATM doesn't have "banker's hours." When you use an ATM, you usually pay a small fee if you're not a customer of that bank chain. These $1 to $3 fees don't sound like much, but they add up quickly. If you use ATMs to withdraw $20, a $2 fee equals a 10 percent charge! The same $2 fee is just two percent of a $100 withdrawal. Try to use your bank's ATMs or those in its affiliated network as often as possible.

Debit cards look just like credit cards but work very differently. Debit cards (also known as check cards) subtract, or debit, money from your bank account just like checks do. Use them at ATMs to get your money from your savings or checking account, and use them instead of cash or credit cards at retail locations, including on the Internet. Many retailers allow you to get cash back (change) when you use a debit card for a transaction.

Since debit cards use a PIN (personal identification number) rather than a photo ID or signature for identification, it's important to keep your number secret.

Memorize your PIN—don't write it down anywhere, especially not on the card! Be careful that others don't see the code when you enter it at the cash register.

A helpful hint from a banker: Select the "credit" option instead of "debit" when you buy gas. Gas stations can put a hold of up to $100 of the money in your account when you use the debit option, and it might be a full business day before they release it. If your balance is low, this can be hazardous to your weekend plans.

U.S. paper money is really made of cotton and linen, not paper. The Treasury Department used to wash and iron currency before putting it back into circulation.

Prepaid debit cards can be very useful for budgeting or limiting spending, or when you don't want to carry cash. They work like gift cards but look just like credit cards. Parents can use prepaid cards to keep some control over your spending or to give you money when you're not nearby.

Money from a bank account or credit card can be loaded (transferred) instantly onto the prepaid card, wherever the card might be. Once you spend the balance on the card, the card can't be used again until it is reloaded. Many locations other than banks sell prepaid cards; be sure to check fees when buying them, because the fees vary widely. Some government agencies use prepaid cards for unemployment and other regular payments.

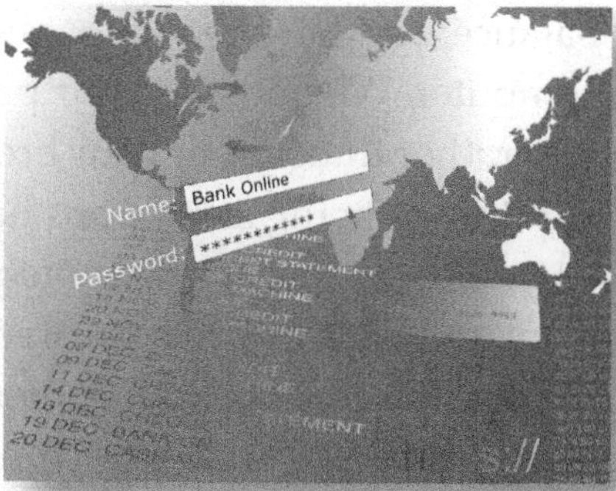

Many banks offer prepaid gift cards which can be registered for extra protection. Prepaid debit cards are especially useful for online shopping because your primary checking account can't be compromised. Bankers recommend that you never use your primary account for online shopping.

Before dispensing paper money in Japan, ATMs press each bill at 392 degrees for 1/10 of a second. The bills come out sterilized and crisp.

Online banking is a great tool to keep track of your money, pay bills, and transfer money between accounts. You can keep a day-to-day eye on your account balance and see when a check clears or a deposit is made to your account. Some banks' online programs even help you create and manage budgets. Anyone with Internet access or a smartphone should make good use of the secure and helpful programs banks offer.

Take some common-sense security measures when you use your computer or smartphone to do your banking. Don't use public wi-fi for banking, even to check your account balance, and be sure you password-protect your phone or computer. When using your phone, use your bank's mobile app rather than using your browser to visit their website. In addition to being safer, apps have some extra benefits; some let you deposit checks remotely once you take pictures of the front and back of your endorsed checks.

Direct deposit is a convenient program preferred by many employers and government agencies because it saves them—and you!—time and effort. Once the paperwork is completed, your paychecks or other payments are credited to your bank account without any action on your part. Some banks even give you free checking if you have at least one deposit going directly into your account each month.

My Credit

Credit is a powerful tool. Manage your credit carefully and it changes your life. Credit can send you to school, buy a house or business, and expand and fulfill your dreams. If you abuse your credit, your dreams and plans vanish pretty quickly, and you find yourself in a deep financial hole.

Your *credit report*, the record of your loan repayment, is reviewed by your prospective employers, landlords, insurance companies, utilities, and other businesses as well as lenders. Financial advisers even suggest that sweethearts review each other's credit scores before marrying! The world looks at your credit report as a reflection of your reliability and citizenship.

Three national credit agencies assign numerical scores based on your credit report, ranging from 300 to 850 (higher is better). The scores boil down a lot of financial information on your report, including late payments, disagreements over billings, and ratio of your debt to your credit limit.

Credit is both a noun and a verb, and the dictionary's long list of dynamic and desirable definitions includes "influence and power."

Borrowers with good scores are rewarded with lower interest rates and preferred terms on loans. A black mark on your credit report will linger there for many years. You're allowed to request a free report from each bureau once per year. Review your report carefully and dispute and clear up incorrect information.

Credit Cards

Credit cards are one of the newest types of consumer credit, in existence for just over 60 years. The very first credit card charge was made on February 8, 1949, when the three founders of Diners Club charged a meal at a restaurant in the Empire State Building in New York City. Before then, people had to pay cash, write checks, or open a separate charge account at each place where they did business.

For the last six decades, credit cards have become an important part of many people's lives. Cards became remarkably easy to get, and even teenage students and people without jobs received credit card offers in the mail. By 2013, college students racked up an average of $3,173 in credit card debt before they graduated.

In 2010, new federal regulations tightened credit card practices and made it harder for people to get credit. Some of the rules were designed especially to protect younger people. If you are under 21, you must prove your ability to repay the loan or supply a cosigner before you receive your own credit card.

One of the helpful new rules requires creditors to include information on your monthly credit card statements about how long it will take to pay the card's balance if you make only the minimum required payments. It's a real shocker to learn it takes 10 to 25 years to pay off your card!

Statements also specify how much you need to pay monthly if you plan to pay the balance within three years. (We'll talk more about balances in Money Math, chapter 4.)

Establishing Credit

Your own bank is a logical place to start your quest for credit; after all, your banker already has a relationship with you. Gasoline company credit cards are also good starter cards. Gas cards are among the easiest to qualify for, though their interest rates are pretty steep. Make sure you pay the entire balance on your gas card every month.

You can look for cards that give you incentives or "thank you" points, but don't pay an annual fee for your first card. There are plenty of "free" cards available. Most of the reward cards that give you points toward airline tickets or monetary awards charge hefty fees.

If you are careful for the first year you have credit, making prompt payments and keeping your balance under 30% of your credit limit, you will be well on the way to establishing good credit.

Identity Theft

In late 2013, debit and credit card information was stolen from 40 million Target customers. Hackers broke into Target's computer system the day before Thanksgiving. From then until Target finally shut them down the week before Christmas, the thieves captured magnetic strip data and PIN numbers when customers swiped their cards and entered their PINs at the cash registers.

The damage was minimized because the customers were told of the theft, their cards were replaced and they were offered free identity protection programs. In most cases, however, identity thieves aren't detected for weeks or months. The average loss per victim in 2012 was $5,000.

Identity thieves do more than just run up your credit card debt. They steal money from your bank accounts, and they open charge accounts and new bank accounts in your name. They can rip off your credit rating as well as take your money.

Professional ID thieves can do a remarkable amount of financial damage by knowing just three bits of information about their victim: birthday, sex, and zip code. Do not tell friends your PINs or loan them your cards. Even if you're confident your friends would never steal from you, they may be careless with your PIN or card.

Gangs of professional ID thieves use many subtle and tricky e-mail scams, such as phishing, to entice you to reveal passwords and personal information. Never send account or password information to e-mail contacts or use account links sent to you within e-mails.

People under 25 years of age are most at risk of ID theft because they are less likely to know their account balance, review their bank or credit card statements, or request a free annual credit report. Statistics show that most young people don't discover they are victims for 132 days, while older people find out in an average of 49 days. Thieves can siphon a great deal of your money from your account if you give them an uninterrupted four months!

Some ID thieves practice a classic hit-and-run technique, cleaning out your account or maxing out your credit card within an hour or two. More subtle thieves will buy an inexpensive item or make a small withdrawal from your account to see if you notice. Once thieves are confident that you're not checking your account, they will milk it dry for an average of five months.

Managing Credit

You can do several things to keep your credit under control and build a stellar credit rating.

Imagine that you're paying cash. It's been proven that people spend 20% more when purchasing with credit or debit cards rather than cash. Don't fall into the trap of thinking you're not spending real money. You are—and it's your own money!

Know your credit limit and your balance. Every month, look at your credit card billing statement and your bank account balance. Sign up for online statements so you can check by phone or computer more often than monthly. You don't want to incur fees for going over your credit limit or for bouncing checks. *Overdraft protection* is a line of credit that your bank establishes to pay checks or debit charges when you're out of cash. It sounds great, and it is, but there are fees and interest payments—plus you have to pay back the money! Your credit card may offer balance alert notices, based on a dollar amount or percentage of your credit limit. Sign up for them if they're available.

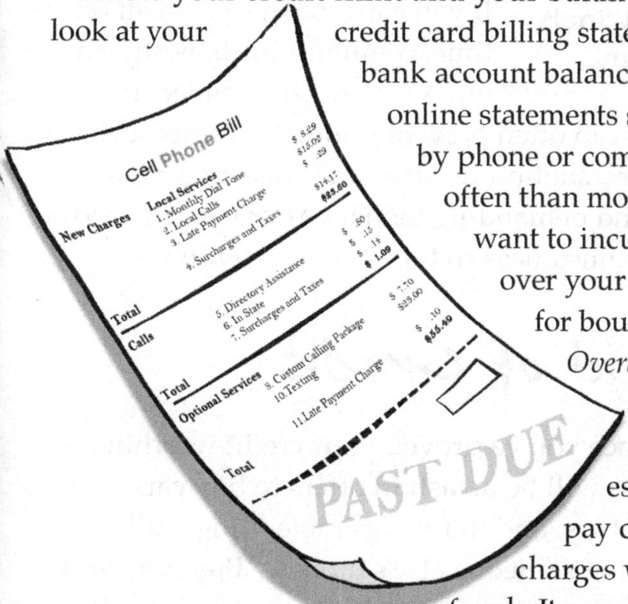

Pay more than the minimum due. If you're familiar with the power of compound interest, you will understand that if you have the unfortunate habit of making only minimum payments, your debt load will skyrocket faster than you can possibly imagine. Pay off the entire balance every month if you can. If you can't pay everything you owe, pay the balance as quickly as possible.

Don't ignore your bills! This is vital if you're having trouble paying them. Remember that your lenders want to work with you. Yes, they want to be paid, but they also want to keep you as their customer. If you can't make a payment on time, communicate honestly and quickly with your lender. Your good relationship can often prevent traumatic events such as repossessed cars, shut-off utilities, and collection agencies *dunning* (calling and demanding money). Your lenders need to know your circumstances so they can work with you.

Use a U.S. quarter as a miniature ruler; it is exactly 1 inch in diameter.

The World of Credit

Once you've proved your credit-worthiness, you will be awash in offers to buy cars, clothes, and many desirable things--all using someone else's money. "Buy now and pay later" is a motto that has woven itself into our everyday lives. This is the perfect time to return to the basics: Make your budget, set your spending and saving goals, and save for what you truly want.

MoneyMath

Review Abby Dinero's paycheck stub on page 11 and her budget on page 22. *For answer key, see page 62.*

1. Abby's budget calculates her income based on her
    - a. gross pay
    - b. withholding
    - c. take-home, or net, pay
    - d. hourly rate

2. Abby's paycheck shows that her federal income tax is calculated
    - a. at 6.2% of her net income
    - b. at 22% of her gross income
    - c. at 10% of her gross income
    - d. at 1.45% of her net income

3. When Abby buys clothes, the money comes from her budget's
    - a. income category
    - b. discretionary category
    - c. balance category
    - d. savings category

4. To pay for her gasoline, Abby works how many hours per month?
    - a. 21 hours
    - b. 17 hours
    - c. 5 hours
    - d. 42 hours

5. If Abby cuts her driving by 10 miles per day, how much discretionary income will she have per month?
    - a. $42
    - b. $80
    - c. $126
    - d. $142

6. Abby's hours are cut back to 10.5 hours per week. How much can she deposit into her college savings account each month?
    - a. $52 if she doesn't spend a penny on herself and all other expenses remain the same
    - b. $115 if she cuts her driving in half and all other expenses remain the same
    - c. answers a and b
    - d. none of the above

7. Monroe's parents co-signed for a credit card with an annual interest rate of 20%, and she used it to pay for a trip over spring break. Her trip cost $1,000. If she does not use the card to buy anything else, how long will it take her to pay for her trip if she pays $40 per month to her credit card lender?

   a. 2 years and 9 months
   b. 1 year and 6 months
   c. 4 years and 2 months
   d. 6 years and 2 months

8. How much interest will Monroe pay over this period?

   a. $204
   b. $490
   c. $24
   d. $304

9. If Monroe increases her monthly credit card payment to $100, how long will it take her to pay off her spring break trip, assuming she charges nothing else on the card?

   a. 10 months
   b. 11 months
   c. 12 months
   d. 15 months

10. With a $100 per month payment, how much interest will she pay?

    a. $52
    b. $104
    c. $20
    d. $200

11. Bill Fold buys a diet drink every day from the mini-mart near his home; it costs $1.50. If Bill works a minimum wage job, how many hours does he need to work every year just to pay for his Cokes? (Hint: minimum wage is $7.25 per hour; calculate withholding at 25% of his gross pay).

    a. 26 hours
    b. 52 hours
    c. 80 hours
    d. 101 hours

How to Balance Your Checking Account

Whether you write paper checks or use a debit card, you should always know the balance in your checking account. Your ATM and debit card transactions immediately affect your balance. Paper checks that you write can take days or weeks to clear—but you need to deduct them from your balance at the time you write them. To know the true balance in your account, add deposits made after your statement is printed and subtract any debit card transactions or checks that you've written.

Let's balance Abby's checking account. Her statement was dated five days ago, and she wants to make sure she knows her exact balance right now. Her paycheck was automatically deposited three days ago, and she's used her debit card for gas and other purchases in the last five days.

1.	List the balance shown on the statement:			$60.00
2.	List the deposit that does not appear on the statement:	Date	Amount	
		5/12	$123.66	+ $123.66
3.	Subtotal of #1 and #2.			= $183.66
4.	Add outstanding checks, transfers, debits, purchases, and withdrawals that do not appear on this statement:	Date	Amount	
		5/11	$22.00	
		5/12	$ 9.00	
		5/13	$72.40	
	Total of #4			–$103.40
	Subtract #4 from #3 to find Abby's current balance.			= $80.26

12. Let's look at Abby's bank statement. If her paycheck had not been deposited,

    a. her account would have a balance of $183.66.
    b. the check she wrote to the insurance company for $72.40 would bounce.
    c. her account would be overdrawn.
    d. both b and c are correct.

13. What's the maximum debit card purchase that Abby can make right now?

    a. $60 b. $123.66 c. $183.66 d. $80.26

14. Monroe is planning another spring break trip for next year, but she's not allowed to use her credit card this time. She decides to set a short-term savings goal and scale back the trip budget to $400. Spring break is 6 months away. How many dollars does she need to save per week for next year's trip?

    a. $15 b. $30 c. $25 d. $10

15. If Monroe pays $100 per month on her credit card bill, needs $40 per week for spending money, and is saving for next year's trip, how many hours does she need to work at minimum wage each week to make her goals? (Hint: Remember to allow 25% for withholding.)

    a. 12 hours b. 15 hours c. 18 hours d. 40 hours

16. Tim Buck worked for a landscaping company during his summer vacation. The landscaper hired Tim as an independent contractor rather than as an employee, which means no taxes or other deductions were withheld from his paycheck. What should Tim do about paying his taxes?

    a. He shouldn't worry and just spend his paycheck.
    b. Tim should set aside 7.65% of his salary to pay the employee half of FICA taxes.
    c. Tim had better save 25-35% of his salary to pay both portions of the FICA taxes plus local, state and federal income taxes.

MANAGING MY MONEY

Saving and spending money wisely are skills that you can develop. You can learn to make good financial decisions that positively affect your future and open doors to new opportunities.

The recession that began in 2008 caused many families to re-evaluate their spending and saving habits. More parents began to share financial information with their children, including them in joint family decisions about vacations, major purchases, and savings goals. If your family openly discusses financial matters, you're fortunate. You have a head start on learning strong money management skills.

If you already save money, congratulations! Set some long-term and short-term savings goals and keep up the good work. Create a budget and continue on the path to financial security.

If you are usually broke, owe money, or don't know where your last dollar went, now is the perfect time to turn over a new leaf and start developing good money habits.

Self-knowledge is the first step to building better money management skills. Understanding what motivates or frightens you about money can be helpful. If your parents are one paycheck away from financial disaster, your money comfort level may be very different from that of someone who made regular deposits into her savings account from the time she was a toddler.

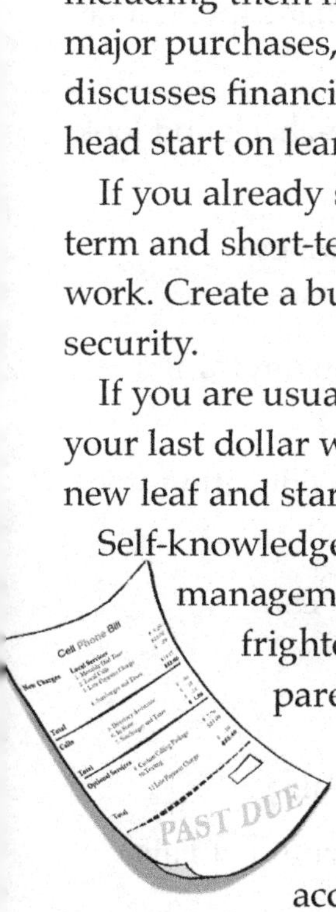

Before you fill out the budget and savings worksheets in this chapter, take the money self-evaluation quiz and discover what type of saver and spender you are right now.

Self-Evaluation Quiz

1. I know how much money I have in cash and in my bank accounts.
   ☐ True ☐ False
2. When I earn money or am given a gift of money, I put 10% into savings.
   ☐ True ☐ False
3. My spending habits won't change when I get a credit card. ☐ True ☐ False
4. I know how much money I spend and what I spend it on.
   ☐ True ☐ False
5. When I buy something expensive, I price-check and look for bargains. ☐ True ☐ False
6. I buy presents for others with my own money.
   ☐ True ☐ False
7. My money is all for me—I can spend it on anything I want. ☐ True ☐ False
8. My parents expect me to help pay for my education.
   ☐ True ☐ False
9. My parents expect me to help pay for my car.
   ☐ True ☐ False
10. I earn my own money. ☐ True ☐ False
11. I have a savings account. ☐ True ☐ False
12. My parents give me an allowance. ☐ True ☐ False
13. I do these chores ____________________________________

____

______________________________ to earn my allowance.

14. My parents expect me to pay for ______________________ ______________________________________ with my allowance or earnings.
15. I donate _______ % of my money to church or charities.
16. If I were given $1,000 in cash with no strings attached, I would do this with the money:

    Spend this amount $________ on this item:____________ ____

    Save this amount $_________ for this purpose: ________ ____

    Donate this amount $_________ for this purpose:____________________________________

Look closely at your answers. Are you generous? Stingy? A saver? Do you spend every penny you have? Do you think about your future, or are you focused on what you want right now?

Savings Goals Worksheet

Long-term savings goals keep your savings program on track; it is much easier to continue saving regularly when you know exactly what you're going to do with the money. Your first long-term goal should be something important and expensive that you want in the future. Two to ten years is a reasonable time period to save for your first goal, though some people save for many decades for a house, their retirement, or their children's college funds.

Choose your first goal to enrich your life or give you life-long memories. Ideally, your goal shouldn't be edible, wearable, disposable, or have a brief shelf life. Some goals might be a car, travel, education, a computer, golf clubs or snowboarding equipment, a horse, or furniture for your first apartment.

My first long-term savings goal is____________________

____

Estimated cost $______________________________________

Date that I want to reach this goal: ____________, 20___

I have _____ years and ______ months to save.

I need to save $_________ per month, $________ per week to reach my long-term goal.

Ask your parents, grandparents, and other adults who give you birthday and holiday presents to give you money for your savings account rather than gift cards or other presents. When they realize that you are committed to saving for something that is important to you, they may help you reach your goal.

While setting a lofty long-term savings goal is exciting and important, you should also set some goals that are achievable in a few weeks or months—definitely less than a year. Let's set two **short-term savings goals** that will reward you for your savings efforts.

Some short-term goals are clothing, a phone, a concert, a day at an amusement park, an accessory for your car, or electronics. They should be things you want but can't easily afford to pay for now. Commit to putting a portion of your earnings, allowance, or monetary gifts aside for your goals. Don't borrow the money to buy them, charge them, or ask other people to buy them for you.

Short-term savings goals	Cost	Weeks to save	$ per week
____________________	$______	______	$______
____________________	$______	______	$______
Plus my long-term weekly savings amount			$______
Total of my long-term and short-term goals			$______

My income is $______________ per week, so my savings will be _____ % of my income. I will need to find $________ additional money each week to meet my goal.

How can I earn additional income? ______________________

____

What expenses can I cut or reduce to help me reach my weekly savings goal?

Items	Amount	Items	Amount
______________	$______	______________	$______
______________	$______	______________	$______
______________	$______	______________	$______
______________	$______	______________	$______

Budgeting Worksheet

A budget helps you set goals for your future as well as for your money. Your budget is your roadmap for earning, spending, borrowing, and saving money.

First, calculate your income and describe how you earn it. Add up the wages you earn and any allowance. Multiply your hourly wage by the average number of hours you work per month.

Next, track every expense, even the tiny ones. You will be surprised how your daily small purchases add up. For instance, if you buy a can of soda twice a week, multiply the cost by 8 (soda = $1.25 x 8 = $10). Describe your expenses in the column on the left.

Subtract your expenses from your income. If your income is higher than your expenses, you should have extra money in your pocket every month. If your expenses exceed your income, you will need to earn more or spend less to balance your budget.

SOURCE OF INCOME AND RATE	Monthly income
______________________________	$_______
______________________________	$_______
______________________________	$_______
My total monthly income	$_______

EXPENSES	Monthly amount
FOOD:	
Snacks	$ _______
Lunches	$ _______
Other meals	$ _______
CLOTHES:	
Work clothes	$ _______
Casual clothes	$ _______
Shoes	$ _______
Dry cleaning/laundry	$ _______
PERSONAL CARE:	
Hair	$ _______
Other	$ _______

Cell phone	$ _______
CAR:	
Gas	$ _______
Insurance	$ _______
Maintenance	$ _______
Payments	$ _______
Savings	$ _______
Gifts	$ _______
Charity and church donations	$ _______
Movies/concerts	$ _______
Hobbies/art supplies/gaming	$ _______
School and sports fees	$ _______
Loan repayments	$ _______
OTHER EXPENSES:	
____________________________	$ _______
____________________________	$ _______
____________________________	$ _______
____________________________	$ _______
____________________________	$ _______
____________________________	$ _______
Total monthly expenses	$ _______
Subtract total expenses from total income to show your monthly **budget deficit or budget surplus**	$ _______

If you have money left over, congratulations! You are demonstrating good money management. This is a great time to increase the amount you put into savings.

If the total shows a negative number, review your budget and look for expenses that you can reduce or cut completely. Free online budget programs are available to track your expenses more closely and help you organize your finances.

My Money Journal

Gifts of Money

On these pages, write down the gifts of money you receive from friends and relatives, and check off the box when you send a thank-you note. The thank-you notes may bring you even more money on your next birthday or holiday.

$ ____________ ____________________ ____________
amount | person who gave me the money | date gift received

____________________________________ ☐ sent thank-you note
reason for the gift

$ ____________ ____________________ ____________
amount | person who gave me the money | date gift received

____________________________________ ☐ sent thank-you note
reason for the gift

$ ____________ ____________________ ____________
amount | person who gave me the money | date gift received

____________________________________ ☐ sent thank-you note
reason for the gift

$ ____________ ____________________ ____________
amount | person who gave me the money | date gift received

____________________________________ ☐ sent thank-you note
reason for the gift

$ ____________ ____________________ ____________
amount | person who gave me the money | date gift received

____________________________________ ☐ sent thank-you note
reason for the gift

$ ____________ ____________________ ____________
amount | person who gave me the money | date gift received

____________________________________ ☐ sent thank-you note
reason for the gift

$ ______ amount | ______ person who gave me the money | ______ date gift received
______ reason for the gift | ☐ sent thank-you note

$ ______ amount | ______ person who gave me the money | ______ date gift received
______ reason for the gift | ☐ sent thank-you note

$ ______ amount | ______ person who gave me the money | ______ date gift received
______ reason for the gift | ☐ sent thank-you note

$ ______ amount | ______ person who gave me the money | ______ date gift received
______ reason for the gift | ☐ sent thank-you note

$ ______ amount | ______ person who gave me the money | ______ date gift received
______ reason for the gift | ☐ sent thank-you note

$ ______ amount | ______ person who gave me the money | ______ date gift received
______ reason for the gift | ☐ sent thank-you note

$ ______ amount | ______ person who gave me the money | ______ date gift received
______ reason for the gift | ☐ sent thank-you note

$ ______ amount | ______ person who gave me the money | ______ date gift received
______ reason for the gift | ☐ sent thank-you note

Gift Card Journal

On these pages, write down the gift cards you receive from friends and relatives, and check off the box when you send a thank-you note. Remember, gift cards are money.

$ ____________ ____________________ ____________
amount received card from date card received

______________________________ ☐ sent thank-you note
store/brand

____________ ______________________________
expiration date items purchased

$ ____________ ____________________ ____________
amount received card from date card received

______________________________ ☐ sent thank-you note
store/brand

____________ ______________________________
expiration date items purchased

$ ____________ ____________________ ____________
amount received card from date card received

______________________________ ☐ sent thank-you note
store/brand

____________ ______________________________
expiration date items purchased

$ ____________ ____________________ ____________
amount received card from date card received

______________________________ ☐ sent thank-you note
store/brand

____________ ______________________________
expiration date items purchased

$ amount | received card from | date card received
store/brand | ☐ sent thank-you note
expiration date | items purchased

$ amount | received card from | date card received
store/brand | ☐ sent thank-you note
expiration date | items purchased

$ amount | received card from | date card received
store/brand | ☐ sent thank-you note
expiration date | items purchased

$ amount | received card from | date card received
store/brand | ☐ sent thank-you note
expiration date | items purchased

$ amount | received card from | date card received
store/brand | ☐ sent thank-you note
expiration date | items purchased

Income

Keep track of all the money you earn. You will be surprised how quickly it adds up. If you get in the habit of writing down your income, it will be easy to plan a budget. *See the Budgeting Worksheet on page 42.*

$______ ____________ ______
amount employer/income source date paid

____
comments

$______ ____________ ______
amount employer/income source date paid

____
comments

$______ ____________ ______
amount employer/income source date paid

____
comments

$______ ____________ ______
amount employer/income source date paid

____
comments

$______ ____________ ______
amount employer/income source date paid

____
comments

$______ ____________ ______
amount employer/income source date paid

____
comments

$______ ____________ ______
amount employer/income source date paid

____
comments

$ ____________ ______________________________ ____________
amount employer/income source date paid

____
comments

$ ____________ ______________________________ ____________
amount employer/income source date paid

____
comments

$ ____________ ______________________________ ____________
amount employer/income source date paid

____
comments

$ ____________ ______________________________ ____________
amount employer/income source date paid

____
comments

$ ____________ ______________________________ ____________
amount employer/income source date paid

____
comments

$ ____________ ______________________________ ____________
amount employer/income source date paid

____
comments

$ ____________ ______________________________ ____________
amount employer/income source date paid

____
comments

$ ____________ ______________________________ ____________
amount employer/income source date paid

____
comments

$\$$ ____________ amount | ____________ employer/income source | ____________ date paid

____________ comments

$\$$ ____________ amount | ____________ employer/income source | ____________ date paid

____________ comments

$\$$ ____________ amount | ____________ employer/income source | ____________ date paid

____________ comments

$\$$ ____________ amount | ____________ employer/income source | ____________ date paid

____________ comments

$\$$ ____________ amount | ____________ employer/income source | ____________ date paid

____________ comments

$\$$ ____________ amount | ____________ employer/income source | ____________ date paid

____________ comments

$\$$ ____________ amount | ____________ employer/income source | ____________ date paid

____________ comments

$\$$ ____________ amount | ____________ employer/income source | ____________ date paid

____________ comments

Savings Deposits and Withdrawals

Even though your bank calculates your savings account balance, it's important to keep track of your account balance yourself.

Add the deposits or subtract the withdrawals, then calculate the new balance. When you earn interest, add it to the balance just as if it were a deposit.

____
date

opening balance $__________

____
date

deposit + $__________

withdrawal - $__________

new balance = $__________

____
date

deposit + $__________

withdrawal - $__________

new balance = $__________

____
date

deposit + $__________

withdrawal - $__________

new balance = $__________

____
date

deposit + $__________

withdrawal - $__________

new balance = $__________

____
date

deposit + $__________

withdrawal - $__________

new balance = $__________

____
date

deposit + $__________

withdrawal - $__________

new balance = $__________

____
date

deposit + $__________

withdrawal - $__________

new balance = $__________

____
date

deposit + $__________

withdrawal - $__________

new balance = $__________

date

deposit + $

withdrawal - $

new balance = $

date

deposit + $

withdrawal - $

new balance = $

date

deposit + $

withdrawal - $

new balance = $

date

deposit + $

withdrawal - $

new balance = $

date

deposit + $

withdrawal - $

new balance = $

date

deposit + $

withdrawal - $

new balance = $

date

deposit + $

withdrawal - $

new balance = $

date

deposit + $

withdrawal - $

new balance = $

date

deposit + $

withdrawal - $

new balance = $

date

deposit + $

withdrawal - $

new balance = $

date

deposit + $

withdrawal - $

new balance = $

date

deposit + $

withdrawal - $

new balance = $

date

deposit + $______

withdrawal - $______

new balance = $______

date

deposit + $______

withdrawal - $______

new balance = $______

date

deposit + $______

withdrawal - $______

new balance = $______

date

deposit + $______

withdrawal - $______

new balance = $______

date

deposit + $______

withdrawal - $______

new balance = $______

date

deposit + $______

withdrawal - $______

new balance = $______

date

deposit + $______

withdrawal - $______

new balance = $______

date

deposit + $______

withdrawal - $______

new balance = $______

date

deposit + $______

withdrawal - $______

new balance = $______

date

deposit + $______

withdrawal - $______

new balance = $______

date

deposit + $______

withdrawal - $______

new balance = $______

date

deposit + $______

withdrawal - $______

new balance = $______

Debt

It's good to keep track of money you owe, even if you borrow from your parents or friends. If you pay the money in installments, always record the amounts and dates.

It is also a good practice to keep track of loans you make to others.

$__________ ________________ ______
amount borrowed or loaned | reason for loan | date of loan

____
terms of the loan (interest/payment amount/number of payments/payoff date)

$__________ $__________ $__________
payment made/date | payment made/date | payment made/date

$__________ $__________ $__________
payment made/date | payment made/date | payment made/date

$__________ ________________ ______
amount borrowed or loaned | reason for loan | date of loan

____
terms of the loan (interest/payment amount/number of payments/payoff date)

$__________ $__________ $__________
payment made/date | payment made/date | payment made/date

$__________ $__________ $__________
payment made/date | payment made/date | payment made/date

$__________ ________________ ______
amount borrowed or loaned | reason for loan | date of loan

____
terms of the loan (interest/payment amount/number of payments/payoff date)

$__________ $__________ $__________
payment made/date | payment made/date | payment made/date

$__________ $__________ $__________
payment made/date | payment made/date | payment made/date

$______ amount borrowed or loaned ______ reason for loan ______ date of loan

______ terms of the loan (interest/payment amount/number of payments/payoff date)

$______ payment made/date $______ payment made/date $______ payment made/date

$______ payment made/date $______ payment made/date $______ payment made/date

$______ amount borrowed or loaned ______ reason for loan ______ date of loan

______ terms of the loan (interest/payment amount/number of payments/payoff date)

$______ payment made/date $______ payment made/date $______ payment made/date

$______ payment made/date $______ payment made/date $______ payment made/date

$______ amount borrowed or loaned ______ reason for loan ______ date of loan

______ terms of the loan (interest/payment amount/number of payments/payoff date)

$______ payment made/date $______ payment made/date $______ payment made/date

$______ payment made/date $______ payment made/date $______ payment made/date

$______ amount borrowed or loaned ______ reason for loan ______ date of loan

______ terms of the loan (interest/payment amount/number of payments/payoff date)

$______ payment made/date $______ payment made/date $______ payment made/date

$______ payment made/date $______ payment made/date $______ payment made/date

Glossary

401(k). A retirement program offered by many employers. The employee can elect to have a percentage of income deducted from her paycheck automatically; the amount is deducted before income taxes are calculated, lowering the amount of taxes as well. The money is considered long-term savings, and is often invested in mutual funds.

529 plans. Investment savings plans for college tuition. These state-run plans offer tax breaks to people who deposit money into your college fund. A fee is charged for managing the investment options offered; some are riskier than others..

ATM. Automated teller machine. ATMs allow you to access your bank accounts from anywhere in the world.

Bonds. IOUs given by governments and companies in return for interest-bearing loans. The IOUs can be bought and sold; they also pay interest to the owners. Most government projects are built with bonds.

Budget. A plan for spending, saving, and earning money. Ideally, budgets are balanced (income equals expenses, including savings). When you spend more than you make, you're running a deficit.

CD. Certificates of deposit are "time deposits" that you make with banks. You agree to leave your deposit in the bank for a specific amount in time in return for guaranteed interest.

Debit cards. Plastic cards that look like credit cards, except they debit, or subtract, money directly from your bank account. A PIN is used to authorize expenditures instead of your signature.

Discretionary income. Money left over when all your fixed (necessary) expenses are paid.

FAFSA. Free Application for Federal Student Aid—a form that should be filled out when you're in high school and every year you're in higher education. It determines your eligibility for federal and state grants, federal student loans, and many scholarships.

FICA. Federal Insurance Contribution Act. Deductions are taken from your paycheck, currently 6.2% of your income for Social Security and 1.45% for Medicare.

Gross income. Wages earned before taxes or other payroll deductions are taken.

Medicare. A health insurance program for disabled or retired workers. The premium is deducted from your paycheck.

Mutual funds. Shares of investments, or portfolios, put together by companies that specialize in researching and buying stocks and bonds. The majority of stock market investors buy shares in these portfolios instead of buying shares of individual stocks.

Net income. Also known as take-home pay; your earnings after all taxes and payroll deductions are subtracted.

PIN. Personal identification number used to access your bank accounts. It should be guarded and never written on your ATM card.

Securities. Stocks, bonds, and mutual funds purchased by investors.

Social Security. A government program that offers disability and death benefits as well as a retirement pension. Employers and current employees split the cost of the premium.

Stocks. Ownership of shares in a corporation. Two types of stocks (preferred and common) have different ownership privileges. Some shares offer dividends, or profit sharing. Stockholders can usually attend a company's annual meetings and vote for the board of directors. Values of stocks can change dramatically depending on the general market, the financial health of the corporation, and public relations.

Withholding. Payroll deductions such as income tax, insurance premiums, savings plans, loan repayments, unemployment tax, Social Security, and Medicare.

Answer Key

Chapter 4: Money Math, pages 37–40

1c (take-home, or net, pay). Plan your budget to reflect the money you actually receive. There is a major difference—usually at least 25%--between the amount you earn and the amount in your paycheck.

2c (10% of Abby's gross income). Abby's paycheck on page 8 includes a listing for federal withholding, which means "federal income tax." The percentage of money withheld depends on the information you put on your W4 form when you're hired. Abby chose to have very little withheld.

3b (discretionary income, or category). Clothes are not part of Abby's fixed expenses, such as cell phone bill, car expenses, etc. "Discretion" is defined as individual choice; Abby chooses how to spend the money in this category.

4a (21 hours per month). Abby works a full week to pay for her gasoline. Remember, she's paying for it with her take-home pay, not her gross income.

5d ($142 in discretionary income, up from her current $80). Gas is expensive!

6c (answers a and b). Her college savings will be cut back to $52 if Abby's hours are cut and she doesn't adjust her budget.

7a (2 years and 9 months). That's painful, but it'd be much worse if Monroe just paid the minimum credit card payment of $26.67 per month; it would take her 117 months (almost 10 years) to pay for her spring break trip. Monroe would pay $1,056 just in interest alone—her trip would actually be paid for twice.

8d ($304 in interest on her $1,000 loan).

9c (12 months).

10d ($200). Monroe pays two extra months of payments to cover one year's interest on her debt (20%).

11d (101 hours). The yearly cost of Bill's daily soft drink is $547.50, and his take-home pay is $5.43 per hour.

12d (her check would bounce and her account would be overdrawn).

13d ($80.26 is Abby's balance)

14a ($15). $400 divided by 26 weeks.

15b (15 hours per week). $15 saved for her next spring break trip, $25 per week ($100/month) to pay off the credit card for her last trip, and $40 for spending money—divided by her wages ($7.25/hour x 75%).

16c (save 25-35% of his salary to pay taxes). Painful but true. If you work for yourself or as an independent contractor, you pay 15.3% of your salary (both the employer's half and the employee's half) of Social Security and Medicare taxes. You must pay from your own savings since nothing is withheld from your paycheck.